Includes Five SAT Words to Know
MEETS STATE AND NATIONAL STANDARDS
Australia
The Land Down Under for Mates of All Ages!
IT'S YOUR WORLD
LIVE WORK PLAY LEARN
Where Do You Want to Go?
Hey! It's the Sydney opera House! Do you want to go?
TIME ZONE • CULTURE • CUSTOMS • CLOTHING • HISTORY
FOOD • CULTURE • CUSTOMS • CLOTHING • HISTORY • LANDMARK
By Carole Marsh

Live • Work • Play • Learn

GALLOPADE INTERNATIONAL

Gallopade International is introducing SAT words that kids need to know in our books. The SAT words in this book have a gray box around them. Students can look up the definitions and increase their vocabulary. Happy Learning!

Gallopade is proud to be a member and supporter of these educational organizations and associations:

Association for the Study of African American Life and History
National Alliance of Black School Educators
American Booksellers Association
American Library Association
International Reading Association
National Association for Gifted Children
The National School Supply and Equipment Association
The National Council for the Social Studies
Museum Store Association
Association of Partners for Public Lands
Association of Booksellers for Children

At the time of publication, all websites referenced in this document were valid. However, due to the changing nature of the Internet, some addresses may change or the content become less relevant.

It's Your World Books

Africa: A Safari Through Its Amazing Nations!

Australia: The Land Down Under for Mates of All Ages!

Canada: The Maple Leaf Melting Pot Country!

China: A Great Wall Runs Thru It!

Egypt: An Ancient Land of Lore; a Modern Land of Oil and More!

France: The Ooh-La-La Country Everyone Loves!

Germany: The Country of Fairytale Castles and Cutting Edge Science!

Greece: A Volcanic Land of Ancient Olympic Origins!

India: Land of Six Senses and Intriguing Mystery!

Italy: The Country of Amazing Fountains and Awesome Arts!

Japan: An Island Country of Endless Intrigue!

Mexico: A Colorful Land of Exotic Culture!

Middle East: Ancient Countries of Current Events Headlines!

Russia: The Great Bear and Its Dramatic History!

South America: A Continent of Countries of Amazing Proportions!

United Kingdom: The Country of Ships, Sealing Wax, Cabbages, and Kings!

Other Carole Marsh Related Titles:

The Mystery of the Great Barrier Reef

Table of Contents

A Letter from the Author

From the desk of
CAROLE MARSH

Hey kids,

It's your world! It really, really is!
Of course, you already know that, don't you?
You surf the 'net, listen to satellite radio, watch television shows and movies set all around the globe–kids today are much more "worldly" than in the past, and that's a good thing!

Now's a great time to learn something about another country–such as Australia. Why? Because one day, you might actually visit there (if you have not already!). You might go to school there–many colleges have ties with international schools around the globe. You might even go on to work in a foreign country!

Many companies have positions in other countries. Companies are "going global" as fast as they can. They have branch offices, manufacturing plants, and customer service centers scattered around the globe!

So, ready or not: YOU are a Citizen of the World! And you'll want to be a good one. How do you do that? You'll find out everything you can about that country, how it's the same, and how it's different from your own country. What language is spoken there? What customs do the people observe? What foods do they enjoy? What do they do for fun? What has happened in this part of the world, and what is happening there now? It's fun ... and the more you learn, the more you will enjoy whatever global opportunity comes your way!

This book is a good place to start your learning journey–so take advantage of the world–IT'S YOUR WORLD, after all ... and guess what? It's a BIG world, after all!

Happy traveling and learning,

Carole Marsh
Always with passport in hand!

Why Should We Care About Australia?

Australia is the only country that is also a continent! Ayers Rock, the Great Barrier Reef, the Sydney Opera House, koalas, and kangaroos all call Australia home. Because Australia is located entirely within the southern hemisphere, it is often called "the land down under." Known for rugged, natural beauty, much of the country is uninhabitable desert. Most Australians live in cities along the vast coastline.

Australia is an important democracy and a friend to the United States and other nations around the globe. Australia's native people, the Aborigines, still live there today. The British first settled the country as a place to keep prisoners. Even after becoming independent, Australia maintained its ties to Great Britain.

One day, you might visit Australia to snorkel along the Great Barrier Reef, pet a koala, or see an opera. It could happen!

Write home about it!
What will your postcard from Australia say?

Top Fast Australia Facts!

Important facts to remember about the country of Australia:

- Australia is officially called The Commonwealth of Australia.
- Australia has a queen, a governor, and a prime minister.
- Australia is governed by its Constitution of the Commonwealth of Australia.
- Australia is one of the major developed countries in the world, active in international matters, and the global economy. It is an ally of the United States and other nations.
- Australia is a founding member of the United Nations.
- Australia has about five million visitors a year.
- Australia is a nuclear power.
- The capital of Australia is Canberra.
- The official language is English.
- The national anthem is "Advance Australia Fair."
- The currency used is the Australian dollar.

Now, you figure out the rest!

1. This is Australia's ____ ____ ____ ____.
2. Australia is an ally of the ____ ____ ____ ____ ____ ____ States.
3. Australia is also called "the land down ____ ____ ____ ____ ____."
4. One of Australia's most famous landmarks is the Sydney ____ ____ ____ ____ ____ House.
5. The __ __ __ __ __ __ __ __ __ __ of Australia is about 21.5 million people.
6. Canberra is the ____ ____ ____ ____ ____ ____ ____ of Australia.

Where in the World Is Australia?

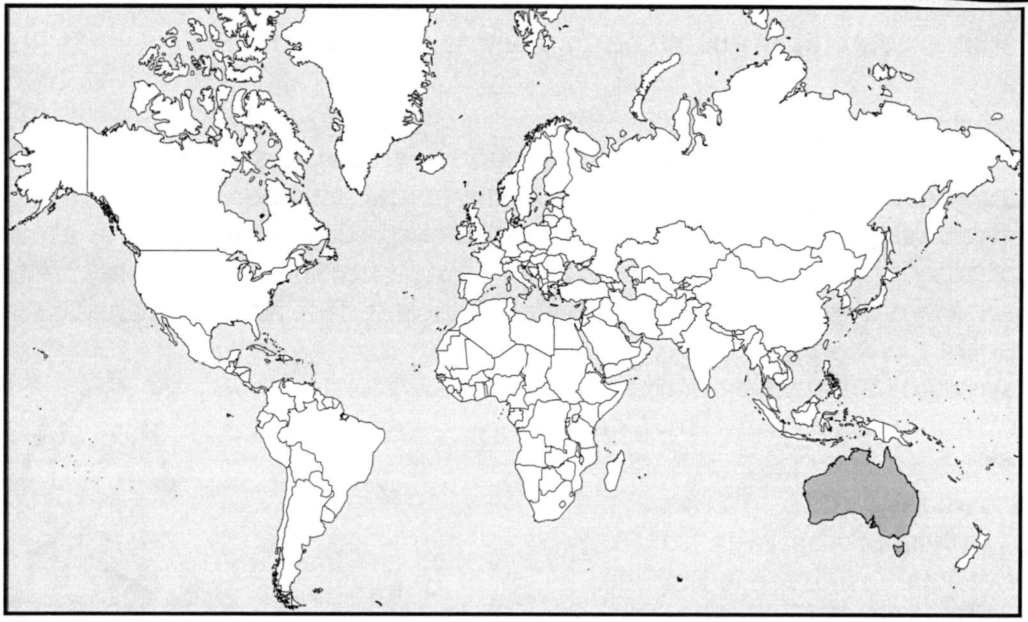

- Australia is located entirely in the southern hemisphere, which is why it is nicknamed "the land down under."
- As an island continent, Australia is surrounded by the Pacific Ocean, Indian Ocean, the Tasman Sea, the Coral Sea, and the Timor Sea.
- Australia has no major rivers to supply water to the inland areas.
- Australia's vast, desert area is called the "outback."
- Australia is the smallest continent but is the sixth-largest country in area.
- The Great Barrier Reef is on the northeast coast of Australia and is the largest coral reef in the world.
- The islands surrounding Australia are often collectively called "Oceania."
- At 7,310 feet, Mount Augustus in Western Australia is considered the world's largest monolith, a mountain made of a single rock.
- Australia is divided into six states and two territories.

Do You Know?

1. The majority of the Australian population lives in the:
   a. outback   b. bush   c. Great Barrier Reef   d. temperate coastal region

2. Indigenous Australians are:
   a. Aborigines   b. Dutch   c. British   d. None of these

Going Once...Going Twice... There It Is!

Have you ever heard the saying, "Third time's a charm?" That saying describes the discovery of Australia! It took explorers three separate journeys to find it!

Early explorers discovered the nearby islands of New Guinea, but somehow they missed the island continent of Australia. It was just 100 miles south! Next, a Dutch explorer sailed around Australia without ever noticing it! Finally, in 1770, Captain James Cook of the British Royal Navy explored Australia's eastern coast. He claimed it for Great Britain and named it New South Wales.

By the end of the 18th century, the British government decided to use the newly discovered territory as a penal colony. A penal colony is a place for prisoners to live.

In 1814, Captain Matthew Flinders was the first to sail all the way around Australia. He was a British navigator and mapmaker. Flinders also helped give Australia its name. The third time was the charm for explorers searching for Australia, the final frontier!

Crosswords!
Use your new knowledge to fill in the crossword puzzle.

Across
3 A __________ explorer sailed around Australia without discovering it.
4 Great Britain originally used Australia as a place to keep __________.
5 Australia is an island, a country, and also a __________.

Down
1 The first explorer to circumnavigate Australia was Matthew __________.
2 __________ is also known as "the land down under."
5 James ________ was the first to settle Australia.

Awesome Aussie History

Prisoners, gold, and aborigines together on an island! No, it's not a reality television show. It's part of the amazing history of the "Land Down Under," which is a nickname for Australia.

Aborigines, the native people of Australia, lived there for about 42,000 years before Dutch explorers discovered the continent in 1606. Aborigines and their descendants still live in Australia.

In 1770, Lieutenant James Cook of the British Royal Navy arrived on the eastern coast of Australia. He claimed it for England and named it New South Wales. It became a prison colony for British convicts! As more of Australia was explored, five more colonies were established. In 1901, the colonies were united and the Commonwealth of Australia was formed!

Australia had a gold rush of its own in the 1800s. People from around the world came to find their fortunes. In the early 1900s, Australia became independent from Great Britain. During World War II, Australia was threatened by a possible Japanese invasion. Australia and the United States became allies during that time and are still friends today!

Today, Australia faces challenges related to pollution, treatment of its native Aborigines, and other modern problems, including the war on terrorism. Despite these struggles, Australia prides itself on cultural diversity, a democratic government, and a strong economy.

Timeline!

Number these events in the order they took place, first to last.

_____ A penal colony is established on Van Diemen's Land.

_____ The Japanese threaten to invade Australia.

_____ Lt. Cook lands on the coast of Australia.

_____ Australia becomes independent from Great Britain.

_____ Aborigines live on the Australian continent.

_____ A gold rush strikes down under!

_____ Dutch explorers find Australia.

Famous Australian Folks!

Matching!

Match these famous Australian people with their accomplishments

______1. A scientist, I won the Nobel Prize for my role in the discovery of penicillin. I was able to help make enough of it to save millions of lives during World War II.

______2. A wildlife expert and conservationist, I am better known by my nickname, "The Crocodile Hunter." I owned the Australia Zoo and also had my own television show. I devoted my life and my work to animal conservation. Sadly, I was killed by the barb of a stingray.

______3. A photographer and an adventurer, I was Australia's official photographer during World Wars I and II. I was the photographer for a team of scientists who explored Antarctica for three years, from 1911 to 1914.

______4. A featherweight boxer, I was originally born in France. I moved to Australia when I was five years old. In 1967, I became the Commonwealth Featherweight Champion. I was inducted into the World Boxing Hall of Fame in 1997.

______5. A lawyer, I have dedicated myself to helping Australia's Tasmanian Aborigines. I was born in Tasmania, and I am Aboriginal.

______6. A cricketer, I am considered the greatest batsman of all time! As a national sports hero, I have appeared on postage stamps and even coins.

A. Steve Irwin

B. Johnny Famechon

C. Lord Howard Florey

D. Michael Mansell

E. Sir Donald Bradman

F. Frank Hurley

Guts and Glory Wonders Down Under!

A. This is a wild dog. It is also called an Australian Native Dog. This animal is usually a reddish color and looks like a mixture of a dog and a wolf. It is a nocturnal carnivore, which means it is awake at night and eats meat.

B. Fleas from infected rats coming from overseas ships brought this to Sydney, Australia in 1900. It killed more than 100 people in about six months. That's not as many as the 25 million it killed in Europe in the 1300s, but that's because there were fewer people in Australia.

C. It was known as a Thylacine, but many Australians called it a "Tazzy." It had stripes on its back and a huge jaw that opened wide, like a snake. Sadly, it became extinct in the twentieth century. It is a symbol for an Australian state.

D. They are Australia's indigenous people. They lived on the continent for 40,000 years before European explorers arrived. After British colonies were settled, many of their population died from disease and from being forced to move. Many descendants survive today.

E. This was the place the British used to house their criminals. It was a penal colony. Criminals were sent there to serve out their sentences and perform hard labor. Australia was originally established as this.

Mixed Up!
Match the paragraph to the word the paragraph describes.

PRISON ISLAND ____

____ **DINGO**

ABORIGINES ____

THE BLACK PLAGUE OF 1900 ____

TASMANIAN TIGER ____

Heidelberg School: Art Down Under!

The Heidelberg School is not a "school" at all! It is actually the name of a late 19th century art movement in Australia. An art critic named Sidney Dickenson coined the phrase when he saw the work of two landscape artists, Walt Withers and Arthur Streeton. They did most of their painting in an area called Heidelberg. After that, any artwork like theirs was thought of as part of the "Heidelberg School."

Artists of the Heidelberg School style painted "plein-air," just as the French impressionists did. "Plein air" means outside or out in the open. These painters were inspired by Australia's natural beauty! Landscapes were popular subjects. Scenes depicting the Australian bush were common. Heidelberg School artists also did paintings that showed simple, everyday life.

Heidelberg School paintings were more than just beautiful works of art. They were important because they offered a history of what life in Australia was like!

Heidelberg School paintings can be found in art galleries throughout the country. In Melbourne, Australia, there is a 25-mile Heidelberg Artist Trail. It is marked with 57 signs. Each one shows a different painting and marks a spot where the artist painted or lived.

Go to (Heidelberg) School!

Get out your crayons. What do you do each day? Pick a part of your everyday life, and turn it into art!

Aussie Animals: Tasmanian Devils, Kangaroos, and Koalas

koala bear

What has a scary screech, sharp teeth, and is found only on one island in the whole world? The Tasmanian Devil! You may know "Taz," as a cartoon character, but Tasmanian Devils are real! They live only in Tasmania, an island off the coast of Australia. These fierce critters are about the size of a small dog. Tasmanian Devils are carnivorous, which means they eat meat. They are also marsupials, which means that after their babies are born, they carry their babies in a pouch until they get bigger.

Another marsupial is the kangaroo, Australia's most famous animal! Most animals walk or run, but kangaroos hop! They have powerful hind legs, big feet, and a strong tail that helps them keep their balance. A baby kangaroo is called a "joey." When male kangaroos fight, it looks like they are boxing! They stand up on their hind legs and try to push each other off balance. Sometimes they kick too!

Koalas are adorable little creatures. Sometimes they are called bears, but that is incorrect. They are marsupials. They feed on leaves from the eucalyptus tree. In fact, koalas spend most of their time in trees and sleep most of the day! They have sharp claws that help them climb.

TASMANIAN DEVIL

Word Play!
Use the letters of Tasmanian Devil to create as many words with three letters or more as you can.

______________	______________
______________	______________
______________	______________
______________	______________
______________	______________
______________	______________
______________	______________
______________	______________
______________	______________
______________	______________
______________	______________

Breathtaking Building!

The Sydney Opera House is one of the most unique buildings in the world! The building's designer received architecture's highest award for his distinctive creation.

The opera house was completed in October 1973. It took 17 years to complete it! The unique shape of the roof was created to save money and time.

Every year, more than two million people visit the opera house for entertainment. Performances range from ballets and operas to concerts. Today, the Sydney Opera House is recognized the world over as a symbol of Australia!

The roofs of the opera house are covered in more than one million white and cream Swedish-made tiles.

Since 1973, when the opera house opened, there have been over 80,000 performances held there!

There is even an Opera written about the Sydney Opera House called "The Eighth Wonder."

The Sydney Opera House uses as much energy as a town of 25,000 people!

The opera house contains the world's largest organ!

Create your very own travel pamphlet. Concentrate on an area that interests you. Perhaps you enjoyed learning about the people. Or maybe it was the animals that interested you. Fold a piece of paper into three sections. This will give you six areas on which to put information.

Do the Opposite!

Customs and culture vary widely from country to country. Sometimes they vary in different regions of the same country. Here are custom and cultural differences observed by the Australians!

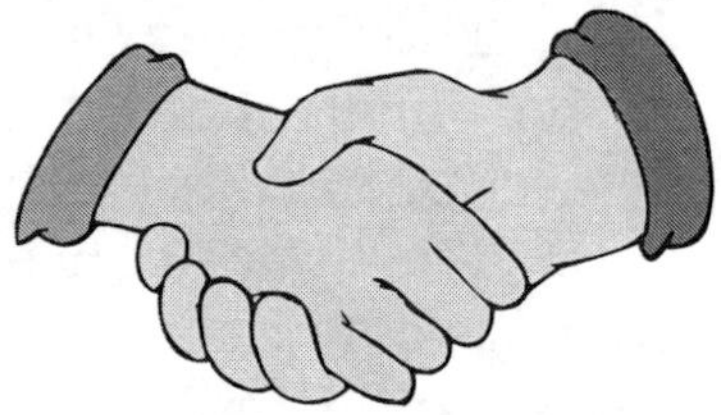

- The handshake is a common greeting.
- People are usually introduced by their first name.
- If you are invited to a "barbie," you've been invited to a cookout! You might be expected to bring your own meat.
- Talking about your successes or achievements is considered quite rude.
- Vegemite is a thick paste made from Brewer's yeast that Australians love to eat on bread or crackers.
- Christmas is celebrated on December 25, which is actually summer in Australia!
- The fork is held in the left hand, and the knife in the right. You hold them the opposite way!
- Australians drive on the left side of the road. It's the opposite in the United States!

Create your own!

As we have seen, customs and cultural activities can help define who we are. Think about your family and friends and come up with some new customs for everyone to try.

They Say What?

The official language in Australia is English, but they sometimes call it Aussie. They may speak English, but some of their words are different.

Match it up!
Below are some common Aussie phrases or words. See if you can match them to the English word.

aggro
barbie
Chrissie
face fungus
g'day
goog
mate
muso
oldies
prezzie

gift
friend
barbecue
parents
moustache or beard
musician
hello
Christmas
egg
aggressive

Happy Holidays!

Australia celebrates many holidays and festivals. Christians observe Christmas and Easter. Australians celebrate New Year's Day on January 1st and the Queen of England's birthday in June.

Australia Day is like our Independence Day, except that it is celebrated on January 26th. This is the day that Great Britain founded the first colony in Australia. Because the Australian seasons are the opposite of our seasons—when it is winter here, it is summer in Australia—they can still celebrate with outdoor events and fireworks, just like we do.

Anzac Day is a lot like our Veteran's Day. It is celebrated on April 25th and recognizes those who served in war. Veterans and soldiers are honored with parades and special services at war memorials.

Boxing Day falls on December 26th. Australians honor service workers, such as postal workers, barbers, and trash collectors. They give these people money as a way of saying, "Thanks!"

Write it down!
Pretend you are visiting Australia. Write a letter to your best friend. Tell him or her what you received for Christmas. Describe what it was like to celebrate Christmas in the summer!

Australia on the Stage and in the Museums!

Australia owes much of its rich cultural heritage to its indigenous aboriginal people. Australia is home to the Sydney Opera House.

1.

2.

Notes

1. The Sydney Opera House is a cultural icon that hosts 3,000 arts events every year.

2. *The Magic Pudding* by Norman Lindsay is Australia's answer to *Alice in Wonderland*.

3. "Waltzing Matilda," by Banjo Patterson, is Australia's unofficial national anthem.

4. The didgeridoo is an aboriginal wind instrument made from hollowed Eucalyptus trees.

5. "Kurntumaru and Parnaparnti," by aboriginal artist Jimmy Pike, tells the dreamtime story of two cousin-brothers.

4.

3.

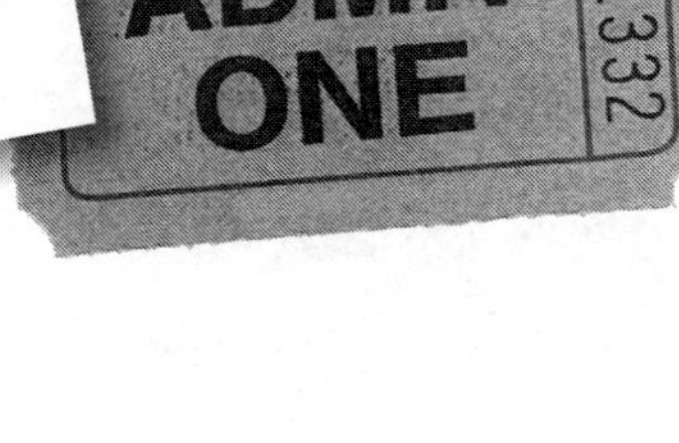

5.

What's for Dinner?

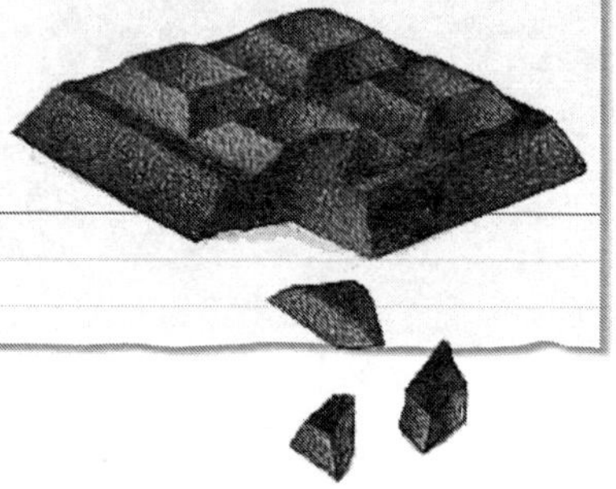

Australian food reflects the country's cultural diversity. Immigrants have brought their cooking methods and dishes with them from their home countries. It is truly a melting pot of cuisine! See just a few of the dishes you could taste if you were to visit Australia.

Billy tea is a strong, black tea that many Australians enjoy.

Anzac biscuits are hard, cookie treats with a gingery taste.

Pumpkin scones are small, flat cakes made of pumpkin. They were brought over by the British.

Wattle seeds are a type of seed that are dry-roasted, then ground to enhance the coffee-like flavor.

RECIPE

Always ask an adult for help when cooking!

Lammingtons

INGREDIENTS

3 cups powdered sugar
4 tablespoons cocoa
1 tablespoon melted butter
1 cup of warmed milk
2 frozen sponge cakes
2 cups coconut

MMMMMMMM...this was good!

DIRECTIONS

1. Sift powdered sugar and cocoa into a medium bowl.
2. Mix together melted butter and warmed milk in a small bowl.
3. Pour the butter/milk mixture into the sugar/cocoa mixture. Blend with an electric mixer until smooth, or for about 3 minutes.
4. Cut the cakes into about 2-inch squares.
5. Dip each square in chocolate mixture.
6. Roll each chocolate-covered square in coconut.
7. Serve lammingtons on a plate. Store extra cakes in an airtight container.

Makes about 20 small cakes.

Cricket—Baseball Down Under?

At first, cricket and baseball might seem similar. Both games are played with a bat and ball, but they are quite different. Cricket is a sport that originated in England. Two teams, each with 11 players, play on a grass field shaped like a circle. In the center lies a strip of ground called "pitch." On each end of the pitch, there are three wooden stumps called "wickets." These are the targets each team guards.

To play, the bowler from one team bowls a cricket ball to the batsman on the other team. The batsman tries to hit it with a wooden cricket bat. The bat actually looks more like a paddle. The batsman tries to reach the wicket on the opposite end to score runs.

There are many forms of cricket. Australia currently has the world's leading team in Test cricket, the highest level of the game. In 2007, the Australian team also won the World Cup for the One Day International (ODI) cricket match.

Figure it out!

Figure out the answers to these questions about cricket.

1. What is the total number of cricket players in the match, counting both teams?

____

2. If one wicket should break, how many wickets remain?

____

Australia plays India at the ODI

Fast Fact:
A cricket ball weighs 5.5 ounces, just a little more than a baseball.

Outback—Not Just a Restaurant!

Maybe you've eaten at the famous restaurant, but that's nothing like the real Australian outback! The large, dry, interior of Australia is known as the "outback." Temperatures can get very hot in the outback's desert-like climate. Most of the land is unable to support crops, but many minerals lie in the ground there.

In spite of the harsh environment, people and animals live in the outback. Many Aborigines, Australia's native people, live there. Dingoes, donkeys, kangaroos, and other animals have adapted to outback life. Fossils of ancient reptiles, mammals, and birds have been found in the outback.

As rugged as it is, the outback is a tourist attraction! The city of Alice Springs is one popular destination. It lies in the center of the continent and calls itself the "heart of Australia." Ayers Rock, also known as Uluru, is a 1,142 foot-tall sandstone formation. It is one of Australia's most recognizable natural wonders. Another unique natural outback attraction is a place called Devil's Marbles. It is named for its huge, round, red granite boulders scattered across a valley area.

Word Fun!

Outback or coastal region? Place the Australian landmark, town, or animal in the correct area below.

Sydney Opera House, Ayers Rock, Alice Springs, most of the Australian population, Devil's Marbles, kangaroos, stingrays, fossils

Outback	Coastal Region

Australia Did It First!

All by Myself!
Herbert John L. Hinkler, an Australian aviator, was the first person to fly solo from London to Darwin in 1928.

Queen of the Track!
Cathy Freeman became the first Aboriginal athlete to represent Australia in the Olympic Games.

I'm Back Where I Started!
Matthew Flinders was the first person to circumnavigate Australia.

He Slides, He's Safe!
The Inflatable Aircraft Slide & Raft was invented by Jack Grant. It is now standard safety equipment on passenger airlines.

Word Fun!

This is fun to do with someone else. Ask a friend for words to substitute for the blanks in the story. Their word substitutions will have a humorous effect when the resulting story is then read aloud.

I want to be the first person to ____________ (ACTION VERB)

across ____________ (COUNTRY)! I've been training for this

since ____________ (MONTH). I'm in ____________ (ADJECTIVE) shape.

My ____________ (ADJECTIVE) adventure will begin on

____________ (FAVORITE HOLIDAY). I won't be hard to miss;

I'll be the one wearing a ____________ (COLOR)

____________ (ARTICLE OF CLOTHING) and a pair of matching

____________ (FOOTWEAR). My faithful friends

____________ (FAMOUS ATHLETE) and

____________ (CARTOON CHARACTER) will be there to cheer for me.

I'm bringing my ____________ (NOUN) along for good luck.

I'm confident I'll be the first!

It's Cold in Here!
The first mechanical refrigeration plant was built by James Harrison in the 1850s.

Copy Cat!
The technology for Xerox photocopying was developed at the University of Sydney by Professor O.U. Vonwiller in 1907.

The Great Barrier Reef, Aussie's Ocean Wonder!

Great Barrier Reef

Australia is filled with amazing natural wonders, on land and in the sea! The Great Barrier Reef is one of them. It lies in the Coral Sea off the coast of Queensland in northeastern Australia. The Great Barrier Reef is the largest coral reef system in the world! It covers about 1,600 miles and has around 2,900 individual reefs. Nine hundred islands are also part of the Great Barrier Reef.

This marine marvel has been called one of the seven wonders of the natural world. The Great Barrier Reef is home to a wide variety of sea life. Whales, dolphins, porpoises, sea turtles, sea snakes, sharks, stingrays, clams, seahorses, more than 1,500 types of fish, and much more live in the Great Barrier Reef.

More than 200 species of birds nest in the area. Saltwater crocodiles slink around in marshes near the reef. The coral is a living thing, too! Four hundred species of hard and soft coral can be found in the Great Barrier Reef. It is a colorful, complex ecosystem!

The Great Barrier Reef is an important tourist attraction in Australia. Nearly two million people visit each year, ready for underwater adventure! They snorkel and scuba dive, exploring the fascinating sights (maybe they're just trying to find Nemo!).

Word Fun!

Interview an expert on the Great Barrier Reef. List your questions below. We've given you an example to get you started.

Example: Where is the Great Barrier Reef?

1. ______________________________?

2. ______________________________?

3. ______________________________?

4. ______________________________?

5. ______________________________?

See a Parade of Penguins—and More!

Penguins prancing about, koalas climbing trees, and seals sunning themselves—these are just a few of the amazing animal highlights of Phillip Island Nature Park! At this Australian park, scientists research, practice, and teach conservation, which is the protection of animals, plants, and their natural habitats. Ecotourism is also part of their work. Ecotourism allows people to visit protected areas and learn about the plants and animals there.

The Penguin Parade is the park's most popular attraction. Little Penguins are the smallest type of penguin. At sunset each night, these tiny "tuxedo-wearing" creatures wiggle their way out of the ocean. Tired from fishing all day, they return to their home on the sand dunes. Park visitors watch from elevated walkways and viewing stands so they don't disturb the birds.

Koalas also have a home at Phillip Island Nature Park. At the Koala Conservation Centre you can see these funny-looking, furry marsupials in their natural habitat. Koalas spend most of their time in trees. Special walkways as tall as the treetops allow viewers an up-close look at the koala!

Named for unique rock formations, the Nobbie Centre is another exciting part of Phillip Island. This marine attraction houses seals, sharks, and dolphins. Thousands of seals—about 26,000 of them—fish and play at Seal Rocks at the Nobbie Centre.

Churchill Island is the historic part of Phillip Island. It is an example of an early Australian settlement. Milking cows, shearing sheep, hand-feeding baby animals, and working dogs are all in a day's work at this historic farm!

Revealing Answer!

Follow the instructions to reveal what "Eco" stands for in the word "Ecotourism."

1. Cross off the first and last letters.
2. Cross off the last letter of the alphabet.
3. Cross off the letter that represents the Roman numeral 10.
4. Cross off the word "IS."
5. Cross off any letter "N."
6. Cross off the letter "D."

REZCXOISLOGNINCDALG

____

Creating One Australia

Queen Elizabeth II

What do the United States and Australia have in common? Each started out as individual colonies that came together to form one nation! Australia began as six different British colonies. After the Australian gold rush, each colony ran its own government. They were still part of the British Empire, but not for long. The settlers wanted to govern themselves!

Great Britain still controlled foreign affairs and defense, but it gave Australians the power to handle their local matters. Aussie settlers also wanted to end the flow of prisoners coming in to the prison colony of New South Wales. In 1848, transporting prisoners to that penal colony ended.

By the end of the 20th century, Australians were talking about unification. They wanted to unite all colonies into a single country. They wanted one government with one constitution for all. The people wrote a constitution that was approved by Britain. On January 1, 1901, Australia became the Commonwealth of Australia. It was an independent nation. Colonies were now states.

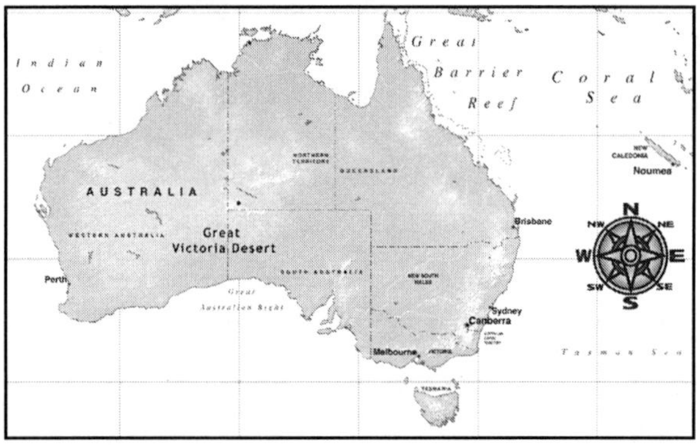

The Australia Act of 1986 officially ended Britain's role in governing the Australian states. The two countries still share one very important thing, though: a queen! Queen Elizabeth II is Queen of England and Queen of Australia!

Cross it off!

Starting with the first letter, cross off every other letter to reveal the name of the native people of Australia.

KAMBROKRSIDGAIUNLEKS

____

Welcome to Sydney!

Sydney, Australia is a great place to live! Sydneysiders, as the people who live there are called, enjoy a good life because of the available jobs, healthcare, education, and leisure activities.

Around four million very diverse people make their home in Sydney. It is the state capital of New South Wales. It has an important history as Australia's oldest city and the place of the first British colony on the continent. It is also the most expensive place to live on the island continent! The one thing it's not, though, is Australia's capital. The capital is the city of Canberra!

Sydney is located on the southeastern coast of Australia. The beautiful city is a popular destination for tourists, and for immigrants traveling to the continent.

Famous Sydney landmarks include the unique, world-famous Sydney Opera House and the 3,770-foot long Sydney Harbour Bridge. The city surrounds Port Jackson, which includes Sydney Harbour. That's where Sydney gets its nickname, The Harbour City. Are you wondering why "harbour" is spelled wrong? It's not! Down under, they spell harbor with a "u!"

Since the Gold Rush of the 1850s, the Australian cities of Sydney and Melbourne have had a friendly rivalry to be the biggest and most important city in the country. First, it was Melbourne, but in the early twentieth century, Sydney took the lead. It was because of this rivalry that neither city was selected as the capital of Australia. The city of Canberra won that!

Figure it out!

List the landmarks and cities that are important to Australia.

S__________

S________ O________ H________

M__________

C__________

P______ J________

N____ S________ W______

S________ H________ B________

Australian Fashion: The Famous Akubra!

Regular folks, prime ministers, and even royalty wear it! From common people to celebrities, the Akubra hat is a part of Australian culture. It is a symbol of the land down under, just like the koala, the Sydney Opera House, or the outback.

The word Akubra (pronounced a-coo-bruh) comes from an aboriginal word for head covering. The hat has a wide brim to help protect wearers from the sun and rain. More than 100 styles of this famous hat now exist. There are Akubra styles for men and for women. One of the most popular is the original style, made of felt. Felt is a light, strong fabric.

This famous head-topper is still made by the family that created it! In 1874, Benjamin Dunkerley started his hat-making business in Tasmania. By 1918, all of the hats his company made were called Akubra. At first, only farmers and others who worked outside wore the Akubra. Today, anyone can wear one!

The Akubra is tough and stylish. It has become a favorite souvenir for tourists visiting Australia. Important officials who visit the country often receive an Akubra as a gift.

Dress Up!

Help Christina get dressed for her tour of Australia. Here are clothing styles you might see in Australia. Choose which outfit she'll wear. Color the clothing, and draw a line from the piece of clothing to Christina, or cut out the clothing and dress her up!

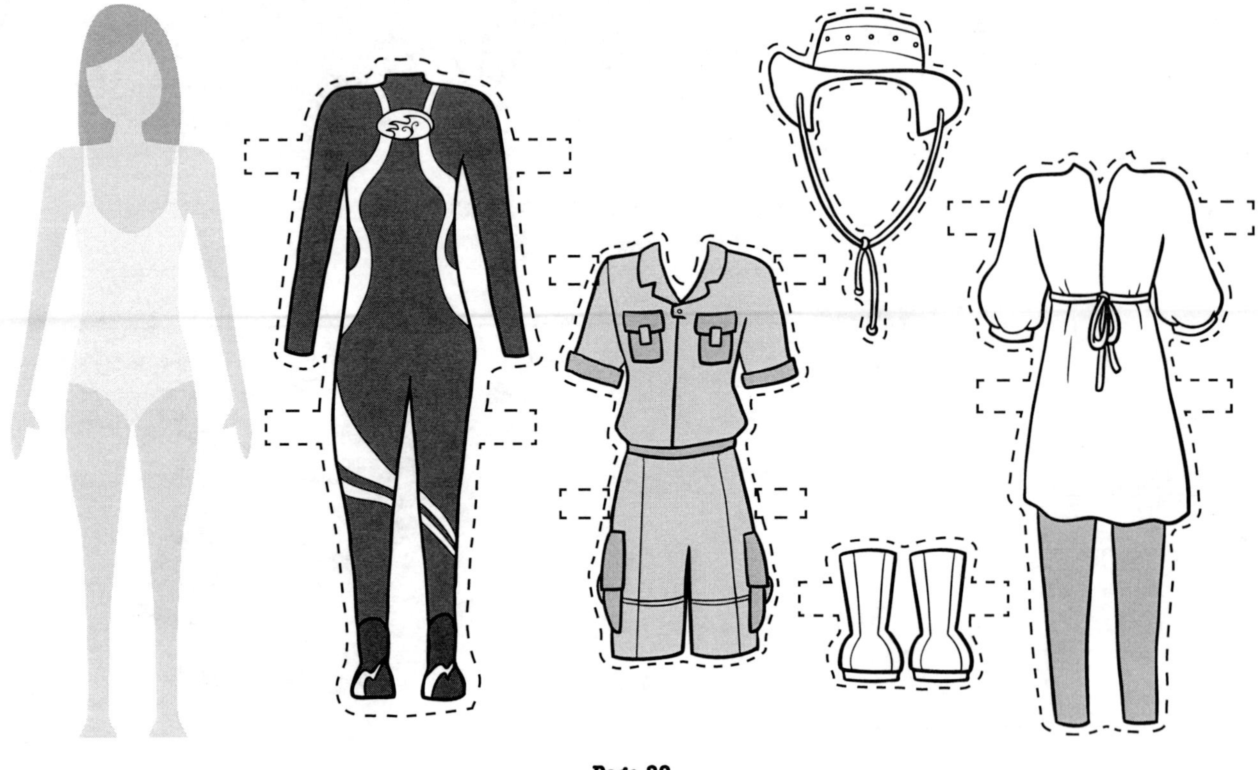

Assorted Architecture!

Figure it out!

Use the following clues to figure out the name of this famous building in Australia.

- It is the second-tallest structure in Australia. The Q1 Building on Australia's Gold Coast is the tallest.
- This structure is 1,001 feet tall, and tourists flock to visit it!
- It took about 11 years to construct, from 1970 to 1981, at a cost of around $36 million Australian dollars.
- At the top, visitors enjoy 360-degree views of the city.
- The city where this structure is located is also part of the structure's name.
- During the 2000 Olympics, it was decorated with sculptures of athletes.

As They Say in Australia...

Figure it out!

Here are a few common Australian terms. You may know some of these words but not the definitions! Why? Because even though Australians speak English like we do, the same word often means something different to them.

Aussie: something Australian

barbie: barbecue grill

bloke: a man

(the) bush: undeveloped, rural areas of the country

cossie (coz-ee): bathing suit

didgeridoo (did-jer-ee-doo): Aboriginal wind instrument made out of wood

digger: an Australian soldier

dingo: wild Australian dog

g'day: good day

mate: friend or acquaintance

minced meat: ground meat

mossie (moz-ee): mosquito

nappy: diaper

outback: dry, remote areas of Australia

Oz: Australia

roo: short for kangaroo

sheila: girl or woman

walkabout: Aboriginal period of wandering in the bush

white ants: termites

____

____

____

____

Can you find four Australian words on your own? Research the internet or look them up in a book. List them on these lines.

Further Resources

Further Resources

U.S. Embassy in Australia
Moonah Place
Yarralumla, ACT 2600
usrsaustralia@state.gov

United Nations
2 United Nations Plaza
New York, NY 10017

Tourism Australia
Darling Park, Tower 2, Level 18
201 Sussex Street
Sydney NSW 2000
Phone: +61 2 9360 1111
Fax: +61 2 9331 6469

Tourism Research Australia
Level 3
11-17 Swanson Plaza
Belconnen ACT 2617
Phone: +61 2 6228 6100
Fax: +61 2 6228 6180

Interesting Websites

www.sydneyharbourbridge.info

http://www.greatbarrierreef.org/

www.sydneyoperahouse.com

www.lakeeyrebasin.org.au

Answer Key

Page 7
1. flag 2. United 3. under
4. Opera 5. population 6. capital

Page 8
1. d 2. a

Page 9

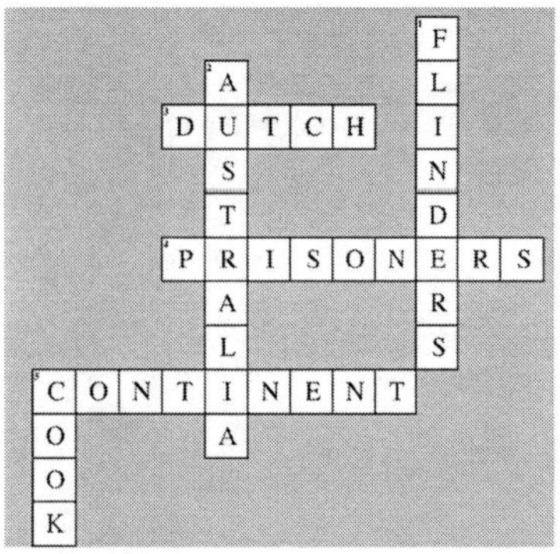

Page 10
4, 7, 3, 6, 1, 5, 2

Page 11
1. C, 2. A, 3. F, 4. B, 5. D, 6. E

Page 12
dingo – A, Aborigines – D, Prison Island – E,
The Black Plague of 1900 – B,
Tasmanian Tiger – C

Page 17
aggro - aggressive
barbie - barbecue
Chrissie - Christmas
face fungus – moustache or beard
g'day - hello
goog - egg
mate - friend
muso – musician
oldies - parents
prezzie - gift

Page 21
1. 22 2. 5

Page 22
Outback: Ayers Rock, Alice Springs, Devil's Marbles, Kangaroos
Coastal Region: Sydney Opera House, most of Australian population, stingrays, fossils

Page 25
Ecological

Page 26
Aborigines

Page 27
Sydney
Sydney Opera House
Melbourne
Canberra
Port Jackson
New South Wales
Sydney Harbour Bridge

Page 29
Eureka Tower